From the Universe in me, to the Universe in you
Love is intertwined through and through
May these poems find a special place in your soul
Together, we'll be whole

For more of Grace, go to: fearlessfreesoul.com

Always
Growing

We All Write Stories

My story is writing itself
The words being my fire's soul
I can never erase
Perfectionism I don't chase
Because what makes the story gold
Are the ups and downs in my world
Loving the character comes easy
When you see the growth
Not all the happy moments
Because then it's just cheesy
THe outside I can't control
But I can live from my soul
Life's path is what I make it
I will keep my true grit
Improve my wit
And always keep my fire lit

My Maze

My mind has many paradoxes
It's like the maze of my soul
Some days, I think I know each hole
The next day, I'm on a new stroll
There is no magical key
Where I'll wake up and know every wave in my sea
I guess that's the thing about this realm
Those at the helm
Don't have the answers
Those around me
Don't have the answers
I AM the answer
As my thoughts and dreams are the dancer
My mind is filled with many curves
Each piece has its purpose it serves
Connected to my being and its nerves
I am not what a version of me deserves
I am the me I choose to be through the power of mind
I am one of a kind
I am my soul and head intertwined
I am the Universe aligned
The stars and voices combined
My head can be blurry and odd
Unpredictable but a channel of god
Alive and abroad
Here's the thing
My mind is always the voice I sing
No matter which way I swing
We're connected though this magical string
Never lonely, it's the Universe I bring

When I Meet You Again

You float in my mind
Like a never-ending river
It sometimes makes me shiver
I wish you could go away
Feeling small
Taking your call
Should've let it go to voicemail
But you left a trail
And I'm following
Since I'm stuck in your trap
Forgetting love's map
When I begin to see again
I beat myself up for being too blind
Looking for love
But instead I watched my eyes find
Fear
Not the first time
Fear used to hold me tight
When I meet fear again
I'll wave goodbye
Remember that it's just a lie
I might say thank you
For showing me the gift of freedom
But I think I'll stick with
Hi and Bye
It doesn't deserve my magic
All those times it convinced me life was so tragic
Yet that wasn't me
It was you
I feel you weakening and trying to grab me too
Bye bye fear
I'll never let you near
The Universe, me
Is always right here

Good Enough

Living for what other people think
Was something I did, and it made me shrink
The Universe and I were not in sync
I never lived for me; this life was but a blink
There was a day I started to realize
There's a difference between caring and disguise
Character and care, are not lies
Putting on different shades and filters isn't wise
Instead, my soul dies
I guess, I also didn't know me through my eyes
Opinions about me and voices in my head
Shaped the me I've now shed
When I started to let go
And give me some attention and care
Life was no longer truth or dare
It became a journey, I was now aware
Judging myself for being the wrong kind of rare
Or basing my personality just to compare
Was more about fear and my little mind's scare
I no longer regret it
If it wasn't for that version of the "someone" I fit
That second wouldn't have split
And I'd still be the fragments coming together
Just to be good enough
Now I'm soft and tough
Alive, free and aware of my magical stuff
I finally chose to be me and broke the handcuff
I became good enough

Cemented Time

Stuck in this fog
My thoughts get stuck in a clog
As if all that surrounded was smog
The same memory comes back
Over and over again
At first it's a strain
But then I soak in the beauty of this stain
See, stains have their wonder
Uniquely shaped like thunder
I let this fog consume me
As if this cemented time
Has me making my way up a nostalgic climb
The laughs and cries soothe my ears like a chime
Then it all stops
And the clouds clear
Now I've made a new memory
Remembering an old one that's in the rear
Hugging my mind for taking me on this journey
While my fears leave on a gurney
This cemented time
Is one I'll revisit again sometime

A Simple Notation

Thoughts are hugging me today
I seem to not want it to go away
Don't know if that's good thing
Or if it's just fear they bring
Either way it has me thinking
Where do they come from?
Are they all mine?
Why the sudden rush?
Should I just press flush?
Or do I let them keep coming?
I'm not running
I like to sit in it
And process bit by bit
A lot of these thoughts
Charge my body with creative juices
No more excuses
I just have to write it down
Some thoughts want me to drown
In a pool of worry
Telling me to hurry
On things in my future I can't control
Like a sickening troll
Then I sit back and release the judgement
It doesn't bring me contentment
This poem might just be my thoughts
On a page
Organizing themselves on this paper's stage
Or maybe it's my fingers' creation
It's probably just a simple notation

Everlasting

When you love
What you do
Who you are through and through
The people who know you
And the dreams you pursue
It's as if time stops
The clock comes to a halt
Moments last forever
The outside world becomes invisible
Love is your driving force
Because you know it's all that exists in this course
You choose to thrive
Because you don't remember how to survive
Now you are alive
There is a burning drive
Inside
Like a fire that doesn't burn out
You've found your route
And all of your doubt
Has flown far away
The true you will always stay

My Heart's Call

Material things started meaning less
On the days I feel a mess
I go looking for my heart's call
My thoughts are running down the hall
That I've created in my mind
But the key to unlocking the door
Isn't picking the best clothes
Or anything that costs more
Than my heart's call
It's funny because no object
Is more expensive than my heart's call
I dig for real conversations
And search my soul for new creations
Or I go inside
And ride the wave of emotion
I'll do anything
As long as I keep my devotion
To my heart's call
The level of illusion these days is quite tall
But on those tough days
I just need to remember my strength
In many ways
My heart is my compass
Lighting the way through the storm
Presenting its love in any form
My heart
I hear you

Eternal Explanation

You ask me
And I answer
Silence becomes the dancer
I smile deep
As this feeling comes over me
So soothing, it puts my worries to sleep
It's this knowing inside
All fear has died
I know who I am
I know what I've been through
I know me to my core
I don't need you to understand
I don't need to explain it more and more
Wanting, wishing and hoping are no longer at war
I am whole, I am proud of me
There isn't a score
The only thing that matters, is my internal roar
All this goes on in my head
As a split second fled
You're still waiting for my elaboration
I'm truly happy deep down, and thanking my foundation
For being my eternal explanation

Truth

Awake

This world
Is full of confusion
Countless things take up your thoughts
The darkness makes sure there is lots and lots
We sleep and wait for something to awake us
But that something has to be you
We choose our reality
For everything is duality
Sleep might be easy
Waking up isn't so breezy
But it is oh so freeing
Our lives are full of illusion
With lots of visits from confusion
But one thing will always be clear
Year after year
We change and we grow
We may hit the lowest of low
But with us awake
Our own truth becomes all that matters
Only we can decide our truth
For your inner voice
Is your choice
And as long as we stand with love
We can all ascend above

Breaking Free

Not much in this world is real
It's not just how I feel
That is just the truth
Our food, air, and water
To name a few
The plan didn't go askew
It was the plan all along
To take away our power
And to take away our ability to question
The truth can be hard to swallow
You can wallow
In the fear
But love is all that is here
It is always near
And the only thing really real
As you read that line
You'll feel
The beat in your heart
Because you are love
You, me and everyone here is love
Love becomes so much stronger
When paired with the truth
Only then do we truly awake
Out of the dream that some don't break
You put love and truth together
You'll be in touch with the Universe forever
Truth will come knocking on your door
Open it and ask for more
Always come back to love
Then tap into truth and rise above
Once you balance this relationship
Of Love and Truth
You'll feel free for the first time
Freedom will have a new meaning to you
I encourage you to remember that meaning
Through and through

Reality Is Dreaming

Reality is dreaming
Truth is gleaming
All externally is a show
All internally is aglow

Reality is dreaming
Let go of mainstreaming
Dive into authenticity
All that's real is inner electricity

Reality is dreaming
Outside is just seeming
All that's deeply honest
Is within, and it's the strongest

Reality is dreaming
What's whole is beaming
Your intuition is your guide
Always truly by your side

Reality is dreaming
There is no redeeming
Mistakes divinely come
Reminding us which journey we're from

Reality is dreaming
No need to be steaming
Anger and happiness are just descriptions
Love is rooted in all your missions

Reality is dreaming
Society is screaming
Begging you to fit in
Instead you rise, fully you with a grin

Reality is dreaming
Illusions are scheming
The Universe chose you
To shine its forever view

Living In Two Worlds

We awake
Out of a dream
Or a different life
Depends on how you see it
And as you sit
Recollecting memories
Shuffling through what stands out
And releasing all your doubt
You stand up
And enter a new world
It could be cold
Or a story untold
No matter what it is
You choose to be bold
Through both worlds you live in
Even if you feel small within
Or that you are just starting to begin
You stand up every day and enter one world
Then you lay down at the end of each day
And enter a new one
For that I hope you give yourself some love
I'll be the little dove
Flying above
Reminding you through this poem
To give yourself credit
For living in both worlds

Float Away

Each breath is a new chance
To give the truth a glance
It all starts with love
You can feel its force above
That something in the air
Love always makes you care
It's not about fair
It's all about feel
Don't let others make you kneel
Stand in your truth
And be who you really are
Fake is not raw
It's just a flaw
Simple to fix
Because love and fear just don't mix
Diving deep in my soul
Until I feel whole
Intuition's on a roll
I see me
I see you
I see truth
I see light
I see darkness
No matter what
I see
And I'm always truly me
Letting this feeling be
Just like a tree
Rooted to my truth, growing each day
Shedding what needs to go
And sitting in the peace
That I am all
Fear will continue to fall
As I listen to my fire's call
Because with the light on
No lies can stay
They'll just float away

Light to Darkness, Darkness to Light

I always thought, something was not quite right
I chose to focus on the light
To evolve and to grow
For I had much of that to do
Woke up from a long sleep
Just a short time ago
Turns out I was right
All the sudden light
Wasn't so bright
Darkness threw me on a ride
Like the tide
It was up and down
Went round and round
Glad I dived in
I won't be the same
I understand this game
And yes, it is oh so lame
But with layers and layers of lies
The world must begin to see
They can't let it be
It is time to unfold the layers
And soak in the truth
It may be painful
But that is your choice
Use your voice
State your opinion
And once your ride with darkness comes to an end
You must Shine your Light
Light is the most powerful
Vibration, Frequency and Source on Earth
Shine
You're one of a kind
With the power of your mind
Courageousness of your heart
Strength of your Intuition
And love and trust in the Universe
Make your light oh so bright

Clue

What if we lived life through the beat of our hearts?
Each beat with its own purpose, its own fire
Then time would be the ultimate liar
The rhythm of our hearts creating life's magical choir
That's our missing wire
The illusion of time and this construct of a world
Teaches us to forget
When our soul and heart first met
The day they came together and created YOU
This whole journey began and was put into view
Maybe this is lifetime #122
Or you're a part of infinity's crew
No matter what, your soul chose to be here
I can feel your smile as you read this loud and clear
Or maybe it's a happy tear
You know deep down you're here for a reason
Not just a lifetime nor a season
Your journey is immortal
This is simply just a test
Rise above the lies, deception and all the rest
Fulfill your mission and do your personal best
You are making yourself proud
Stand apart from the crowd
Do what your soul came here to do
This life is just your journey's clue

Living The Dream

What if I told you this life is imaginary?
A distant vision, a sparkled existence, a perfect temporary
It can be scary
But that's a choice
On the contrary
You can harness your inner voice
The director of this dream
Your eternal team
It's hard to believe this is it
Born, grow up, work and die
It has to be an illusion, a lie
We're here for a reason
Believe in the beyond, look me in the eye
You are more than this human vessel
You are something special
A blazing roar
An adventure to explore
With wings to soar
And love as your core
You're an infinite being
It's freeing
No more agreeing
Let's start seeing
Seeing our soul
Seeing our heart
Seeing our truth
And then feeling
This magical healing
As you start to emerge
Your beliefs will diverge
You'll realize nothing is outside
Everything is within
You're more than skin
You're alive, you're divine
You're whole, you're in control
This is your quest
Let me take care of the rest
Destiny is already coming to be
Wake up and see
You are me

Deception's Lullaby

This world is a dimension of its own
Many things are not known
It's the truth that has not yet flown
Lies sitting on the throne
This deceptive movie being shown
Our reality is not at all what it seems
But it's through love and light where my soul beams
I often wonder if this life I'm living is just a series of dreams
Because I know anything mainstream is just a bunch of schemes
We're tricked and they want us divided in a million different teams
Their frequency of fear hums this corrupt lullaby
But I don't believe in a good or bad guy
I believe in love
And I know fear is the illusion they want me to fall in
I just smile and grin
Because now with my eyes open
And my soul alive and awake
I can hear and watch their lullaby
I'm immune to it, I continue to fly
I have my own bubble
Protected from any 3D trouble
I thrive, fulfill my mission and spread my love double

Love And Truth

Love is an unforgettable memory
A powerful remedy
Infinity's melody
There'd be no love without truth
A paradoxical team
Illuminating reality's dream
With open eyes
And an intuition alive to realize
The world and its real lies
Love can soar
Because together they are more
Truth is powerless without love's flame
Love without truth is simply a game
Intertwined for eternity
Their force is harmony
With an everlasting balance
Even in the silence
You can feel their equal scale
Writing their own tale
Journeying through forever's trail
It's a duality
Driven in immortality
But it's a oneness in all
That answers the soul's call
We know love
It's not below or above
It's within
And when you add truth – they start to spin
The truth is an awakening
It's an inner knowing
Rooted in authenticity
Divinely guided to synchronicity
Sparking this intrinsic electricity
Love and truth's team is always in you
Forever and always, eternally through
Tap into truly being alive, and you'll see from their view
Love is deeper than you ever knew
Truth is a poise you instinctually pursue

To The
Universe

Thank You

Tingling in my fingers
That feeling lingers
Fire inside
Living my life truly alive
Because I realize I am here to thrive
Believing in myself
Knowing I am the stars
And all my scars
Brought me to where I am today
My fear floated away
Forever gone
Freedom engulfs me
That's the feeling I let be
For there's nothing better
Letter after letter
I wrote to the Universe
But I realized it knew it all
The Universe is me
So, all I said was
Thank you

Love's Note

It's always you
Seeing me for me no matter the view
Guiding the way through and through
Ever since we truly met
I can't forget
You're one of a kind
And when the synchronicities align
Your hug gives me the most joy
Today I'm showering you with my love
You're my magical little dove
Always inside, below and above
When I believe, I turn up the heat on our stove
For a while you drove
But then freedom hit and I took the reigns
You're always there to tell me when to change lanes

It's always you
Shining a light on those days I grew
You're my glue
Even when I was scared
You never flew
You've been with me through every lifetime
And will be through every experience that's new
You know it's never been easy
"It" being trust
But you illuminated my stardust
Took away the rust
And taught me how to be free
You gave me the vision that doesn't just allow me to see
But to unlock the truth key

It's always you
Thank you for being my infinite crew
And for being there no matter what life I debut

Of course, I've always been talking to you Universe, me

A Moment With Silence

I sit and stare
Breathing in the crisp air
A moment with silence
Assures me all is well
My worries fly away
Doesn't matter if it's night or day
A moment with silence
Is an escape from the business of my mind
With silence I find
The knowing in me
The knowing that it truly is ok
Everything will be fine
Even if it's not mine
Or the journey isn't a straight line
I know it is all good
That's not just a mood
It's a way of living
A moment with silence
Helps you wave farewell
To those demons inside that sometimes dwell
You can then realize
Worrying is silly
Overthinking is most often a curse
Perfectionism isn't perfect
But you are free
You make your own choices
And listen to your own voices
A moment with silence
Thank you
For the peace and clarity too
I'll always remember you no matter
What form or energy you take
You'll be with me when I wake
And when I break

You're Willing To Bet

You believed in me when I didn't
You nudged me along when I was stuck
I don't think that's just luck
You're the spirit in that duck
And the life force to nature's creation
You're the largest eternal nation
And a piece of you has rested in me
It wasn't until with open eyes I began to see
You challenged me for a reason
And loved me through every season
Just as I planted a seed in your soil
Our connection will never spoil
Like an everlasting love coil
Together we shine
And remind each other we are the divine
I see you in every sign
And feel you in our forever bloodline
Caught in this universal net
From the day we met
To the day this life is set
You're willing to bet

Glazing My Aura

Your touch makes me gasp
Locked your harmony on me like a clasp
It soothes me in ways I'm just beginning to know
Your effortless glow
Captures my soul in this timeless flow
It's funny I'm saying you, when I know it's me
The Universe inside
Is where my love resides
And our magic collides
This world and its divides
Can take us on many rides
But nothing will separate us, we are our own guides
Because we are one
The Universe, my heart, mind, soul, and intuition spun
And turned into this someone
ME
Glazing my aura
Providing me with this eternal plethora
Abundance shall shine
As long as I remember you are always mine
Letting go of you and me, labels get in my way
This authentic sway
Allowed my heart to splay
This glaze on my aura will forever stay

Love's Lullaby

My voice in your head
Lying you down in this cozy bed
We will always be connected through this endless thread
It's you through all these lifetimes I've led
I'm your day and night lullaby
Hugging you through any aching pain
Celebrating all the joys and highs you maintain
Pushing you to grow and fly like a plane
Rocking you to sleep no matter what clogs your brain
And always loving you no matter what stain
Or turn you take on this journey's lane
I was with you from the moment you were born
I will be till the second this life ends
And forevermore
You must trust every here and now
It's not in the how
Or the why or wow
It's in the eternal vow
To remember everything happens for a reason
And is meant to be in your evolution
There are no problems nor solution
Those are just labels of this world's institution
You are here for the truth revolution
Never fear being lonely
I am here and I'm not the only
I surround in everything you see
It just takes open eyes and a loving heart to be
I am your forever voice
Always here, it's not a choice
It's in our soothing lullaby you can hear peace rejoice

The Truth Within

Just the stars and I
No one will lie
Eyes focus on the sky
Mind focuses on the heart
The Universe laughs, it's oh so smart
My mind wonders what's so funny
Then I hear it sweet like honey
It brings a smile to my face
A moment spent with grace
The Universe in me waves at the Universe in the stars
I thank them for my scars
They thank me for creating them to be
They'd be nothing without me
I'd be nothing without them
That is what makes us laugh
To the human in each of us we seem so finite
But to the magic
We know we're infinite

You're In My Head Every Night, Every Night

Memories and flashes
Fire and ashes
Reality crashes
This horizon clashes
The light and the dark
Battle for who makes their mark
The night wins this race
And it's the dream I can't wait to face
I lay my head to rest
Thoughts swirl about today's part in my quest
I feel blessed
Upon this universal test
There are days I ace
There are days I rely on my foundational base
But every day, I have this pillow and bed
Awaiting my head
And a story I haven't read
I enter the dream dimension
My reality's extension
I feel my higher self seeking my attention
Letting me ride this ascension
This cycle repeats
Each time I embrace these warm sheets
The Universe and I have many little visits or meets
Beyond sight
Through light
Quite bright
You're in my head every night, every night

Into Your Arms

Lost in all your charms
Jumped right into your arms
Love's essence was too enchanting
The voices in my head stopped ranting

Words disappeared, worries vacated
Feelings were created
That's how I knew the Universe in me was activated

This day, my soul long awaited
This eternal zone
Is becoming my backbone
I'm no longer alone
With your magic truly shown
Fear is unknown
And so are my harms
Here I am, forever in your arms

The first day I felt truly alive, was the day I ran into your arms
"Your arms", being those of the Universe, me

Together Forever

You were my beacon
As fear's touch started to weaken
I felt your glow
Like the sun's ray
Surrounding my being, above and below
The inner child in me started to play
Becoming free, I saw you
Started in my rear view
Then became crystal clear and oh so true
My dreams were the glue
Tying together love, belief and growth
So, I could break through
You were my golden light, my ground crew
Together we made a great team
The light inside you let me gleam
You weren't fake or a scheme
You were so real, you built my self-esteem
Eased the pain when I wanted to scream
You took me on adventures deep within my soul
Those adventures let me become whole
You and me were on this awakening stroll
But you let go, and became the best I friend I've ever known
You whispered in my ear when we were alone
"I am you, I've been you through every zone"
You unlocked a part of you that had yet to be shown
And now we no longer need to be two
We are one
And with that we spun
Together forever, we began to run

Magical
Sedona

Escaping

I'd rather write poems
I can explore my heart's totems
Add a little mystery to take away the pain
It's freeing to break fear's chain

Another tear with connection
I knew it'd come, just my mind's projection
The second it started, I knew the risk
I let it sting, now I'm ejecting your disc

You're still missing
Our past in my head is hissing
You'll come back one day
It's not you or me to betray

This past week has felt like a year
All these feelings beginning to sear
A wild universal test
A burning in my chest

I'm so ready for an escape
Let me exit this reality, this landscape
Sedona couldn't have come sooner
The rock, the energy, the people
The stars followed by the lunar

I hope to find you there
I know I'll come back a newer version of me
Healing all my scars, letting them repair
This growth doesn't scare
Because I know you are me and we're rare

Grace

I've found my escape
Back to the place
That wraps its energy around me
In a big warm embrace
There's a certain grace
It leaves a trace
On my heart and soul
Makes me feel whole
I hear the voice in my head
Telling me, this is home
As I let my being roam
The trees wave hello
The wind says a silent nice to see you
The mountains enclose me
And I couldn't have more joy about it
For a second, the dream comes to a split
I feel as though this is the only real spot
That's not just a thought
It's a knowing in my gut
I truly feel alive
Like there's no option but to thrive
My mind is a symphony
My heart is smiling
My intuition is talking to me so loud and clear
All fear in the rear
Remembering that this life is for me to ace
I embrace this grace

I've Always Known

Something in my heart changed
The second I entered this vortex, my mind no longer deranged
Light consumed my being, already inspired and refreshed
I asked the Universe for three signs
Instead I found twenty two
That's the magic of this energy, somewhere I always knew
The distant whispers of the trees
The spark in me frees
The weather may be a certain degrees
But the peace in me creates an inner breeze
Watching my brave little dog
Frolic in the water's twinkle and chill
Feeling the enchanting creek's thrill
Everything will be ok
The Universe is visibly more alive
In this electric soul sway
It's always in me to thrive
Basking in the nature
I AM love's creator
This is home
Even when I'm not in this comforting dome
The dreamy memories in my head will forever roam
And so will the vibrations, somewhere in me I've always known

Blanket Of The Night

The electric blue sky
Holds my whispers in the night
Hears my beliefs in the light
Gazing at the stars
Refreshing to hear only the Universe, not even the cars
Found harmony and peace
In this fearless release
The only movie I'll be viewing
Is the magical bubble around me
While my dreams start brewing
Thoughts and worries float away
Love is so vibrant and real
It's all I can see and feel
The buzzing of the crickets gives my senses zeal
As I surrender to the blanket of the dark
And the fire's blazing mark
I lean into the trees and their beloved bark

Magical Twinkle

Sparkle in my eyes
Erasing the world's lies
Including the skies
The special shine in my aura
Due to the miracles the Universe
Has brought to my door
I'm sure it's been here before
And my eyes weren't ready to see
But today I'm immersed in it
Don't know how long this feeling will stay
No matter what I'll always remember
As I savor each moment like the best meal
I've ever eaten
Today I'm not feeling beaten
By the world and its madness
I'm here and alive inside
The twinkle in my soul
Has my vibration elevated
The connection I feel to all
Is answering my heart's call
Feeling so alive and blessed overall
The best part is that I can choose this feeling
Whenever I want
And so can you
The choice is ours to thrive
I know somedays are hard
When you feel so stuck
But rise out of the muck
And come to this side
Don't let fear make you hide
The beauty of this life is the ride
It may seem like our world is only dark
But your spark
Is always
The Magic Twinkle

Here I Am

I wanted to come back a newer me
I think I did that, and I hear my heart agree
Love is all there is, the rest can just be
Still waiting for answers on a few things
But the unknowns are no longer caging my wings
The creator in me sings
Already been tested a few times
Turn it into rhymes
Like a net, they landed on me for a bit
I felt it, I'll admit
But I let it bounce off
Listened to my gut, tapped into my spirit
My destiny is always mine, already formed
It's sunlit
I am the director
And the projector
Happiness is my navigator
Love is my narrator
Dreams are my illustrator
Fear is never my dictator
My soul is my equator
There's a balance in the air
This world is a seesaw, not always fair
But definitely worth our care
I cherish this trail
With freedom I set sail
And with fearlessness I will never fail
For it's an illusion, and I'm in charge of perception's scale

Riding My Waves

The Stream That Pours Through Me

Words, my biggest gift
And curse all in one
Use them till my head spun
Only then do I realize
I miss them
When they come in heaps
It's time for me to make leaps
Sometimes I can
Other times I ran
I could write till the end of time
Sentence after sentence
And the words would still flow
Like there was no drain
Ideas come as if it was pouring rain
My soul never feels the strain
Although words sometimes are a curse
Bringing up things I'm not willing to face
Or burdening me with things I need to live
For you can't write what you won't do
I keep writing for you
That person inside
Who feels a little more sane
When the words meet the page
Words
You're like me
Helping me grow into who I want to be
But sometimes being too hard
On that person who's just trying
To be the light in the storm
But I see you in every form
I know you'll keep coming
And I sincerely thank you
For the stream that pours through me

Still Thinking

I let my thoughts wander in my head
Before I went to bed
Guess I took some to my dreams
Showing me things
I don't know I want to see
Not that it's all bad
Just the uncertainty
Sometimes drives me mad
It is indeed you I see
Will these dreams come to be?
Or is it footage just clogging my brain
Sinking down an endless drain
Even if it's just a show
Most moments aren't too low
Looking down the row
Of the thoughts you created
Down the hall of my mind
I watch the Universe
Pick which past or future to show
No matter what
It always shows me something that's good
Somedays I wake up steaming
Somedays I wake up gleaming
Somedays I wake up dreaming
I could live in the dream instead
You confuse me
Because I wonder why you still take space in my mind
But you I enjoy seeing
I just wish you were still being
And you I ask to see
So, thanks for coming to be
I see the signs
All the different kinds
This poem was supposed to bring me clarity
But that's a rarity
So, I'm still wondering
Will some of these dreams come true?
Or is it just a show of my ever-changing point of view?

A Late Night's Musing

Beauty is within never outside
Let love conquer, let it reside
The Universe, me, is the ultimate guide
I look up at the stars and they tell me
"Destiny and freedom will forever collide"

Things that mean the most to me
Are the hardest to see
The longest process, an eternal plea
There's freedom in trusting and letting it be
I know I'm not there yet, but, through this journey of growth
Someday connection and I will agree

We're all weird
In a good way, not something feared
As pain seared
We evolved and grew, past selves disappeared
Here we are, proud and alive, illusion has cleared

I trust in the divine
Acceptance and passiveness is a fine line
I'll always let my soul and heart align
And with that I'll hear the secrets of the Universe
It's my choice to shine
I let love rule and trust intertwine

Piecing Us Together

What if I had changed?
What if you waited too long?
And the me you knew had gone?
Would it have hurt or burn?
Or would it have just been a lesson to learn?
I was there waiting at every door
Said the twists and turns in my core
You took me on adventures to soar
Thought you let me fall when I needed you most
I saw you on the coast
And you whispered that you were there
While the wind blew through my hair
I ignored you, because your voice hit me like bricks
I thought you were playing tricks
And then you appeared in that dream
I guess you know me too well
I don't even know why I was mad
Or maybe it was the distance that made me sad
I wished you could've just sped things up a tad
I know everything is meant to be
But why does time have to become a lost key?
I fell into my little mind's game
But it's not me I'm going to blame
I've done it too much to make that move again
Instead, I let it go and thanked you
Turns out, we're always learning something new
I remembered my perception can sometimes be askew
My impatience doesn't need to turn into a mental zoo
Alternatively, I can look through the eyes you view
While I put my trust to the test and collect what's true

I Hear You

Trigger after trigger
Makes my ears ring
Taking a deep breath
I stay grounded
My heart well rounded
Understanding different opinions
But rooted to my own
Sitting in my energy zone
Feeling my mind and my soul alone
Words come and go
Feelings bring me joy and woe
Heart continues to pound
But I'm always listening
To what he says
Or she says
But mainly to what I say
It's all that matters
Triggers can try their best
But I will conquer and let them rest
All will work out
I shall not pout
Right now, it might hurt
But I'll get up
Cause that's all I can do
Always knew
There'd be these days
Where I'd feel tossed around in many ways
But that spirit inside is alive
It never dies
Pain doesn't scare me
One + One, Two
Pain + Love, I grew
The point of the Universe's test
Is to not fall into stress
Remember I'm blessed
This is all part of the quest
I'm not mad at him
Or her
It will all be fine
I'm just listening to the voice that's mine
This much is true
Because I hear you

Blank Screen

I spend more time staring at a blank screen
Then I ever did in a previous life scene
Maybe I'm waiting for your name to pop up
Or for the poem to just write itself
My thoughts jump off the shelf
Arrange themselves on this blank sheet
Tug my rubberband cause you're in my head
Waiting for my dream and I to meet
Then words and I can intertwine our thread
So much in the air
It's hard to know which thought I want to make concrete
Too often I jump in and care
Practicing protecting my heart, regret and I don't need to re-meet
So much to write about, how will I ever get it all out
I guess that's what writing is about
A beautifully weaved route
Never a drought
On the contrary, something I can't live without
Staring at a blank screen
Is when my daydreams are seen
More alive than they've ever been
I imagine seeing your name
All my words breaking the frame
I imagine the screen having a vivid image of my inner flame
Hearing this reality's game
When I close my eyes and see this blank screen
It's you who's there, how keen
Define "keen" how you like, it's more than it appears to mean

Fateful

My soul knows
I can feel it in the way
Energy flows
The chirping crows
Make me howl
My heart starts to growl
My circle keeps me going
Lots of ups and downs
My mind goes through so many rounds
Connection lets me feel
What's real
And teaches me to grow
With all the different lights in my life
We help each other glow
To you, I'm here
And to you, let's spiral out of our reality sphere
My circle, I am eternally grateful
The rest is so fateful

You and Me

I'm sitting right next to you
But you're in a world far away
And I'm in my own soul sway
You're sitting right next to me
And we're talking
But you know the difference in our attention is shocking
Or maybe our mouths are talking, while our thoughts are walking

I'm drafting a message to you
And maybe you're doing the same
I keep some to myself, for they are feelings I don't know how to tame
You're soaking in the words
Like the distant chirps of little birds
Then you write me back
As I feel your energy hit me with an exciting whack
We go back and forth
And our realities mix for a time
Then we swim back into our own paradigm

I'm looking at you
And your eyes meet mine
But the swirl in our heads and hearts don't align
Like different ends of the same twine
Our emotions soak in this Universal brine
And we hope for the day when the same star will let us shine
I'm writing this
So are my other dimensional selves
Multiples of me surround, like books on a plethora of shelves
We come together
And drift apart like a floating feather

Isn't funny how two people can be doing the same thing but in such totally different worlds of their own?

On My Mind

Sometimes I wish I knew the future
Other times I enjoy the mystery
I do hope the future isn't history
I see miracles and love
Not this game that continues to float above
I'm ready for the truth to come out
When will people take that route?
I'm ready for new beginnings
And fresh perceptions
Not all these misconceptions
Patience has never been my friend
But trust will be there till the end
Learned many lessons with the Universe
It's always there and it will always stay
It's not going to leave in May
The Universe will love
And be with me
For the rest of time
Cause I am it
And now I can't make these lines rhyme
That's my cue that this piece is complete
Set in stone, it's concrete

Uniquely Me

It's Crazy

Thoughts come down like pouring rain
It's crazy

Something burns inside, so alive the label might be pain
It's crazy

In love with life, I let miracles flood
It's crazy

My words drop onto the page like blood
It's crazy

Something's not right, my feet are stuck in the mud
It's crazy

Time to jump and run, this life is what my soul chose
It's crazy

Memories surge and synchronicities flow, as if time froze
It's crazy

Growth is the journey of my soul, I'm learning to appreciate the lows
It's crazy

I see and hear but, I'm realizing it's the connection to all I'm starting to feel
It's crazy

Excitement for life tingles through my being – something so real, maybe zeal
It's crazy

So many emotions in this human experience
It's crazy

Flavor

I could be bitter
I could be sweet
I could be salty
I could be your treat
I could be whatever you want me to be
It's all perception
I know who I am
And that's no misconception
I hope you'll see me for me, the light
But even if you don't, won't be crying at night
I'm so proud of me for knowing my flavor
Each piece of me I savor
And if you don't appreciate my taste
My time I won't waste
No hard feelings
We're not supposed to be on this path
It's simple math
1+1 isn't 0, it's 2
The Universe is right on que
I see me through and through
Someone will too
And they'll become my crew

Knife

Isn't it funny when you're with someone and their voice goes blurry, all you can think about is that someone who makes you worry?

Isn't it funny when you're split in two, the creator and the bystander seeing life through our view?

And then that song comes on and you realize something is wrong.
This has to be a vision or some type of hidden prison.
A complex part of life – one true friend and a knife

A knife to cut the lies
A knife to cut fear's cries
A knife to know what this place is
Or if it's all just a quiz

When we think of a knife, we think of pain and something sharp or dark.

How about something crafted and created, smooth and weighted?

Maybe it's sharp just like us all.
We have our light and our darkness.

Our darkness is just as beautiful as our light, because without it magic would have no sight.

You're Probably Right

Life is short, you're probably right
Life is more than this lifetime, you're probably right
Your destiny is in your hands, you're probably right
Your dreams only remain dreams, you're probably right
You are a fragment, you're probably right
You are the infinite Universe, you're probably right
Love is all there is, you're probably right
This reality is just an illusion, you're probably right
I am your mind's eye, you're probably right
I am who I choose to be, you're probably right
Because whatever you believe, you're probably right